Y0-BTU-533

CLOUD AND WATER
An Interpretation of Ch'an Poems

———————————————— ■ ————————————————

By Venerable Master Hsing Yun
Translated by
Fo Guang Shan International Translation Center

HSI LAI UNIVERSITY PRESS
LOS ANGELES, CALIFORNIA

Hsi Lai University Press

First Edition 2000
Printed in Los Angeles, United States of America

ISBN 1-929192-03-7
Library of Congress Card Number 00-101400

Cover designed by Shih Mei-Chi

Cloud and Water: An interpretation of Ch'an poems; translated by Fo Guang
Shan International Translation Center

   p.   cm.

1. Religious life - Buddhism
   I. Fo Guang Shan International Translation Center.
   II. Title

<u>Content</u>

Foreword

■

Acknowledgements

■

I. Philosophy of Life

II. On Practice

III. On Mind

IV. Ch'an World

Foreword

In this book we have a collection of Ch'an poems; Cloud and Water. What do we mean by cloud and water? Clouds float by water flows on. In movement there is no grasping, in Ch'an there is no settling. The cloud and water life is a life of living in the moment, always fresh and ready to experience. These poems have been grouped together because of the tone and feeling that they share. Many of these poems were set down by celebrated masters, while for others their authors remain unknown.

Master Hsing Yun has given a brief commentary on each of these verses, giving us the benefit of his many years of deep practice and insight. The commentaries contain many stories and even new verses of their own which shed light on the meaning of the poems. The poems and the commentaries offer a glimpse of Chinese culture and in particular how Buddhism came to be expressed through the many aspects of Chinese society throughout the ages. With his down to earth comments, Master Hsing Yun has been able to show the relevance of these poems to everyday life, and the universality of Ch'an.

Acknowledgements

We would like to express our appreciation to those who contributed towards this publication. Special thanks to Ven. Tzu Jung, Chief Executive of Fo Guang Shan International Translation Center for her guidance; Amy Lam, Jeanne Tsai, Maria Niu, Robin Stevens, Corey Bell, Colin Batch and Emily Lui for their translation and revision; and Shih Mei-Chih for her artwork and cover design. Their valuable contribution has made this publication possible and is most appreciated.

I. Philosophy of Life

◆

*"Worldly ups and downs
should be treated
As lightly as the clouds
gathering and breaking up"*

◆

Good deeds
stand tall like a green pine,

While evil deeds bloom like flowers.

It seems
the pine is not as brilliant as the flowers.

When the frost comes,
the pine will still stand tall,

While the flowers,
withered, can be seen no more.

This little poem artfully highlights the principle of cause and effect. Good deeds can be compared to a pine tree. When we do a good deed it may not attract much attention, whereas evil may at first seem appealing. When the time of retribution comes, goodness, no matter how plain, will beget goodness while evil will only bring about ruin and demise.

Let us use another example. Evil can be compared to a grindstone. When we use a grindstone everyday we do not notice it getting used up, until one day we realize it has become much smaller. Evil people are like the grindstone, you do not see from the surface that it is being worn out, but actually it is wearing out daily. Good people are like the orchid, you do not see it grow, but actually it is growing everyday. If you do evil deeds, do not imagine no one will find out. You cannot escape from cause and effect or even your own conscience.

So do not worry about not getting good results for the moment. Just look at the flowers and grass in the garden. It seems you cannot see them grow, but bit by bit, they come to full blossom. There is a saying which goes, "When one is kind others take advantage of him, but the heavens will not. When one is evil people are afraid of him, but the heavens are not." So we do not have to be too calculating about gain and loss for the moment because karma works across three lives, past, present and future, never failing.

In ancient China, a young man went to the capital to take a civil examination. When the examiner was correcting his paper, he noticed that one of the characters was missing a dot. However, as he was about to deduct points from the exam score, a group of ants gathered at the place where the dot should be as though trying to hide the error. The examiner tried to shoo the ants away. As soon as he used his hand to brush them away, another group of ants gathered at the same place. He was surprised and asked the student if he could explain this phenomenon. The student then told him that once while he was studying, he noticed a group of ants searching for food, not only did he not brush them away but out of kindness, he fed them a candy.

As you can see, his kindness to the ants was rewarded, cause and effect never fail.

Our conscience will tell us
if we are really good or bad,

We don't have to ask what is the cause
of our bad luck or good fortune.

There is no escape from
 the law of cause and effect,

It is just a matter of
time before the effects will come.

"Our conscience will tell us if we are really good or bad." Others may not be able to tell if we are really good or bad, but we ourselves will know. Also, heaven and earth will know. We cannot escape from cause and effect. Thus, *"We don't have to ask what is the cause of our bad luck and good fortune."* If we really want to understand what is the cause of it, we do not need to turn to others. All we have to do is ask ourselves. We reap what we sow. We plant our own causes and reap our own effects. There is an old poem to this effect:

> *If we want to know what are the causes in our previous lives,*
> *We are living the consequences of those causes.*
> *If we want to know what our future lives will be like,*
> *All we have to do is look at what we are doing today.*

Some may have doubts in the law of cause and effect. They may see some really nice people fallen into hard times, while some crooks are not punished and seem to have everything going for them. What they did not know is that it is the working of cause and effect.

Why are some nice people in hard times? The reason is they have not exhausted their bad karma from previous lives. It is just like paying off an old debt! Then why are some sinister people enjoying a good life? The reason is they have not exhausted their good karma from previous lives. The law of cause and effect spans three life times: the present, the past and the future. *"There is no escape from the law of cause and effect; it is just a matter of time before the effects will come."* Some plants yield fruit every year. If we plant this type of plants in the spring, we should be able to harvest in the summer; some karma will manifest in this life. Some plants take two years to yield any fruit; some karma takes two lifetimes to manifest. Some plants take many years to yield any fruit; some karma takes many lifetimes to manifest.

There is no uncertainty in the law of cause and effect; it is just a matter of time. I just want to offer this piece of advice. Good people should not get frustrated if they did not see any fruits for their good acts. Sinister people should not think that they are lucky for not getting caught, for their time will come. There is no escape from cause and effect.

You ride on a horse,
while I ride a donkey.

Looks like you are better off than me!

Turning around, I see a man pushing his
cart.

Some are better off than me,

But there are others less fortunate than
myself!

In this world, we should not compare ourselves with other people. If we do, we will be constantly frustrated. We should not be too calculating also. People who are overly calculating are constantly in a tug of war with others and can never find peace.

"You ride on a horse, while I ride on a donkey." You can always find someone better off than yourself. You drive an import while I drive a domestic car. You drive a car while I only ride a motorcycle. You ride a motorcycle while I only ride a bike. But, *"Turning around, I see a man pushing his cart."* There are lots of people who do not even own a bicycle and they have to walk. We need to understand that although there are others more fortunate than ourselves, there are also many who are less fortunate. We need to be content with our own situation and not always expecting more. If we must compare, we should not compare ourselves in the areas of wealth, fame, and luxury. Instead, we should compare in the areas of ethics, abilities, knowledge and forgiveness. We should better ourselves in these areas.

The verse above tells us to be content with our own situation. Let me tell you of a verse mocking people who are never content with themselves:

At first, I work hard for two meals, then it is for nice clothing
Now that I have nice clothing, I long for a beautiful wife
Now that I have a beautiful wife, I want a nice carriage
Now that I have a fleet of nice carriages, I want a fertile farm
Now that I have many acres of fertile land,
I want a government title to impress others
I do not want to start at the bottom of the ladder,
not even in the middle
When I am at the top rung, I want to be the emperor for a while
When I am the emperor and everything is going well,
I long to live forever
There is no end to my wants, until the day I die with reluctance.

You can tell from this poem that there is no end to our wants and cravings. One's happiness does not hinge on how much money one has or what title one carries. Sometimes, money can bring you headaches and impressive positions can bring you more worries. We should not be selfish. We should not only take, but also give. Someone who only knows how to take, without giving, will never be happy.

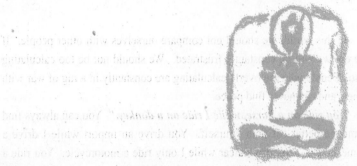

The dragon in shallow water is at the mercy of the shrimp,

A tiger on the plains is chased by dogs.

Relationships are like tides: there are highs and lows,

Worldly ups and downs should be treated

As lightly as the clouds gathering and breaking up.

This verse can be very helpful in our cultivation. Someone may feel that he has been ignored by others. He feels that he is not given the opportunity to achieve his potential. He feels like *"A dragon in shallow water, is at the mercy of the shrimp."* He compares himself to a dragon which is trapped in shallow water. Not only is there not enough water for him to demonstrate his power, he is tackled by the shrimp and fish swimming around him. Thus he harbors ill feelings about others and blames others for not treating him fairly.

"A tiger on the plains is chased by dogs." Someone may feel that he is a very capable person, with the prowess of a tiger. Yet he finds himself not in the forest where he can demonstrate his strength, but on the plains where he is chased by dogs. He blames others for not getting the respect he thinks he deserves. He does not know how to reflect on his life and realize that he is neither a dragon, nor a tiger. He is just an ordinary person like you or me. If he can change some of his bad habits and treat others with kindness and respect he can turn the world around, others will in turn reciprocate and gladly make friends with him.

"Relationships are like tides: there are highs and lows, worldly ups and downs should be treated as lightly as the clouds gathering and breaking apart." There is an old saying, "People will travel many miles to visit a rich relative; yet will ignore a poor friend living next door." If you are poor, people may ignore you. One day when you become rich, relatives and friends start to call. This is human nature, and we should not dwell on it. What we should do is to look at relationships coolly, like the drifting clouds either gathering or breaking apart. We should not be bothered by it. If we do not become petty, we can truly stay happy.

A few decades ago, Venerable Yuen-ying held a formal teaching assembly. At the end of the session, the monk in charge of calling signals accidentally transported the command's "Hit the teaching master and see the big bell off." (In a formal assembly, the proper etiquette is to sound the bell and "see the teaching master off".) Venerable Yuen-ying promptly replied, "Don't hit me, I can leave on my own." This shows us how he handled situations lightly and with humor. In our dealings with others, if we can use a little humor, we can always turn an unpleasant situation into a happy one.

Life comes and goes like lightning,

Love brings endless suffering.

When one realizes the nature of truth and falsehood,

He will be free from the net of birth and death.

"Life comes and goes like lightning." Our life span is very short, as short as a spark of a flint or a flash of lightning. Even if we live to eighty, to ninety, to a hundred and twenty, our life span in the scheme of the universe is as short as a flash.

Why are we in this rat race? What are we striving for? Besides working for a livelihood, most of our toils are for love, thus we say, *"Love brings endless suffering."* We were born out of the love between our parents. The Buddha referred to us as "emotional sentient beings," because we were born out of emotions. We often cling and grasp to love and emotions - love of our family, love between a husband and wife, even the love of a hobby. Because of our clingings and graspings onto all kinds of love and emotions, we have suffered a lot of pain.

What is love? Why is love so hotly pursued? Is it worth it? To put it bluntly, love is a potion smeared on the blade of a knife. It is sweet, bitter, sour, and spicy all mixed together. One has to risk cutting one's tongue to taste the little bit of sweetness. Some people even risk their lives for love. It is very important that we balance our love so as not to fall into extremes. Nowadays, a lot of young people fall in love blindly. If they do not get what they want, they get angry. Some even commit suicide.

Once I talked to a young man who was contemplating suicide, "Why are you so foolish?" He replied, "She is so pretty; yet she does not love me!" Then I told him, "Why do you torture yourself? Why do you want to commit suicide just because she does not love you? There are more pretty girls than the countless stars in the night. There are lots of other girls that you can fall in love with when the time is right. There is no sense in killing yourself just because of one girl."

True love is as open as the clear blue sky. If we can widen our hearts, there are lots of things we can embrace with love: love of our society, our country, all fellow mankind and all sentient beings. *"When one realizes the nature of truth and falsehood, he will be free from the net of birth and death."* If we can love what should be loved, and let go of what does not deserve our love, then we will not be tortured by love. If we can know the true nature of love, then not only will we not commit any sinful acts, we will also be able to escape from the cycles of rebirths.

Worldly matters come and go
like lightning.

The wheel of rebirth
rolls forward like drifting clouds.

We cannot predict today what will happen
tomorrow,

Where can we find the time to
gossip and criticize?

"Worldly matters come and go like lightning." Wealth and power are impermanent. Worldly matters can change as quickly as a flash of lightning and last no longer than a dream.

"The wheel of rebirth rolls forward like drifting clouds." As we wander from life to life in rebirth in the six realms, we may find ourselves in heaven, we may find ourselves in hell, or among the hungry ghosts or animals. These continuous rounds of rebirth can be likened unto a running stream. Where are we heading next? When will we stop?

"We cannot predict today what will happen tomorrow." Matters of this world change so suddenly and are hard to grasp. Who can know what will happen tomorrow? If we take off our shoes and socks today to go to bed, we do not know whether we will be able to put them back on tomorrow.

"Where can we find time to gossip and criticize?" Life is so unpredictable and ever changing, unstable as a bubble. Truly understanding the impermanence of life, how can we waste time in gossip and criticism.

One day when the famous Ch'an Master Lan-jung was busy sweeping the grounds. He stirred up so much dust that his nose was running and his eyes were tearing. A passer-by suggested that he should wipe away his tears and blow his nose. The Ch'an Master looked at him and told him he was too busy to find the time. Can you imagine the level of focus and concentration that he did not even have time to wipe his eyes or blow his nose?

Life is short. We should not procrastinate. We should do what can be done today. More importantly, we should start our Dharma practice as soon as possible and embark on the path to enlightenment.

Before I was born, who was I?

After birth, who am I?

We come into this world with happiness and depart with sorrow,

Who is the one on the deathbed with his eyes closed?

This verse comes from the Ching Emperor Shun-chi's poem in praise of the monastic order. His questions are aptly put. Do we know where we come from? Who were we before we were born?

The human body is made up of the four elements of earth, fire, water, and wind. When we die, these four elements scatter and are regrouped as we take on another physical form with rebirth in one of the six realms of existence. We are lost as we move from one realm to another. We do not know what we are doing in the womb, and when we are born we do not know who we are. Most people rejoice at births and lament upon deaths. What is true joy? What is true sorrow?

Once, a Ch'an master was going door to door to seek for alms. It happened that one of the families he visited just had a new baby and everyone was congratulating the new father. The Ch'an master, however, started crying out loud. The new father was very surprised and asked him why he was crying. He replied that he was crying because there would be one more death in the future.

Birth comes from death. If we do not want to die, then we must make sure that we break the cycle of rebirth within the six realms of existence. Once there was a famous poet, by the name of Po-hu Tang, he wrote this poem to illustrate the brevity of life:

It is rare that we live to be seventy,
And my seventy years come as even a surprise to me.
The first ten years of life we are too young to know anything.
The last ten years, we are too old to do anything.
This leaves only fifty good years, half of which we spend in sleep.
This leaves us only twenty-five years to truly live.
But do you realize how many obstacles
We have to endure in these twenty-five years?

Nowadays people can live to be a hundred and twenty. In the boundless life of the universe a hundred and twenty years go by in a flash. Not to mention many of us will not live to be even a hundred. Many will pass away in their sleep, and we are never sure if we will continue living from one moment to the next.

The joys of birth and the sorrow of death are normal emotions for most people. But someone with wisdom will not allow this precious life to go by meaninglessly. They will not allow themselves to wallow in ignorance. We must beware of delusion and open ourselves up to understanding life and death.

When people slander me,
what should I do?

Forbearance is the path of least harm.

Set a good example for
my children and grandchildren;

Follow the gentle, not the violent.

We should not get too upset when slandered by others. It does not hurt us too much to get the short end of the stick once in a while - for when the clouds clear, the sun will shine through. We need to treat others with sincerity and honesty, thereby setting a good example for the younger generations. Even further, we need to *"Follow the gentle, not the violent."*

We should be reasonable when someone slanders us. Once slandered it appears we are getting the short end of the stick. This is not true. In reality, if we can be patient and uncalculating, if we refrain from seeking revenge, in time people will know the truth. Then the slander not only will not harm us but will become an opportunity to gain merit.

Just as the *Sutra of Forty-two Sections* says, "To slander others is like blowing dust into the wind; not only will it not harm others, the dust will ultimately fall back on ourselves. To slander others is also like spitting up into the sky, when it falls, it will fall flat in our face." Thus, we should not be bothered by others' idle talk and slander. Instead, we should be tolerant, patient, and forgiving. The greatest strength in this world comes not from fists nor guns but from tolerance under insult. According to Buddhist teachings, the merit gained from practicing the precepts is not as great as the merit gained from practicing tolerance. So you can see here the strength of tolerance.

In our practice the first thing we need to learn is tolerance. We have to be tolerant in our speech and should not yell at others for no apparent reason. We have to be tolerant in our bodies and should not show anger on our face. We have to be tolerant in our minds and be truly forgiving of the bad deeds that others have done to us. If we can do this, we set a good and invaluable example to the younger generations.

There is a story in the *Sutra of the One Hundred Parables.* One day, a father sent his son to the market to buy some food and drinks to serve his guests. When his son did not return for a long time, the father was getting worried and went out to look for him. He found his son standing on the street staring at a stranger. The father was puzzled and asked him why he stared so. The son told his father that since the stranger would not step aside to let him pass, both of them decided to stare at each other to see who would give up first. The father was very mad and told his son to run home with the groceries and he would take his place and see who would win.

Does not giving a single step mean victory? Does this make us truly happy? If we want to set a good example to the younger generations, we should be tolerant, patient, and forgiving. Our children will benefit from it tremendously.

If you don't consider your affairs over three times you may regret it.

If you can do this then you don't need to worry about future problems.

All things go by with time like the flow of water.

Everyday our mind could be as light as the spring winds.

We have to think things through thoroughly and be careful in our actions. If we were impulsive, we would surely regret it for many circumstances require tolerance.

Once there was a merchant who planned to go home for the New Year celebrations. He wanted to buy a present for his wife. He lingered around the market, and stopped in front of a monk who sold Buddhist verses. Out of curiosity, the merchant stepped forward and asked the monk, "How much is it for a verse?" "Ten taels of gold." "That much?" the merchant exclaimed. "The verses are very accurate. Surely they are worth the price." The monk replied. The merchant thought for a while and said, "Then, I would like to buy a verse." The monk then read the verse and asked the merchant to memorize it very well.

A verse only consisted of four sentences and it cost him ten taels of gold, the merchant was somewhat regretful yet he knew it was not proper to show his reluctance. He traveled day and night till he reached home. When he arrived it was already midnight of New Year's Eve. He saw that the front door was not locked properly. He entered and proceeded to his living quarters with wonder. In the dim light, he saw a pair of men's slippers. Enraged, the merchant thought, "My wife has cheated on me while I was away." He went into the kitchen and picked up a knife and went directly back to his room. In the heat of the moment, he remembered the verse from the old monk.

Take three steps forward and think,
Then take three steps back and think again.
If you want to know truth in life
The thieves of the six roots are accomplices in crime.

The wife of the merchant was awakened by the noise of his stepping three steps forward and three steps back again and again. She was elated to see her husband yet was confused by his rage. She was overwhelmed after she learned of his accusation. She said, "Ai Ya! Today is New Year's Eve. You were not home. I placed a pair of your slippers to bring about good luck for your safe return." Her reply hit the man like a clap of thunder. He exclaimed with joy, "Ten taels for the verse was worth every bit!"

In our daily living, we must realize that what we see with our own eyes or hear with our own ears is not always in accord with reality. We can easily be deluded by the six roots which are accomplices in crime. Therefore we must be cautious.

II.   On Practice

◆

"It is after bone-chilling cold
That one can become a king
of the Dharma."

◆

A face with no anger is a true offering,

A mouth that speaks no anger is fragrant and fresh.

A heart with no anger is a priceless treasure,

Buddha nature is beyond time and limit.

We have to be watchful of our anger. In Buddhism, anger is compared to fire because it can negate our good karma. When the fires of anger come, they quickly burn down the forest of merit that we have worked so hard to cultivate.

Thus we have to control our anger. First, as mentioned in the opening, *"A face with no anger is a true offering,"* we should keep smiling. One of the most beautiful things in this world is a smile, and it is one of the best forms of charity and benevolence. Some people mistakenly think that one has to be rich to be charitable, they do not realize that a genuine smile to others is not only a most valuable form of charity but also a wonderful offering.

In Buddhism, there are many forms of charity and benevolence. We can donate food, clothing, furniture, and medicine. We can also offer incense, flowers, fruits or valuables. We can use our body, speech and thoughts to make offerings. The highest offering comes from the heart. The heart's true happiness is shown by the smiles on our faces; that is the best offering.

"A mouth that speaks no anger is fragrant and fresh." When we talk, we should do so kindly and sincerely. We should not disparage, nor slander. We should not gossip or talk behind people's backs. As it is said in the *Diamond Sutra*, the Buddha only spoke the truth, and did not engage in exaggerations and lies. Talking kindly is like a breath of fresh air.

"A heart with no anger is a priceless treasure." We need to watch diligently to make sure anger does not arise. We should show no anger on our faces, use no angry words, and go to the bottom of our hearts to root out all thoughts of anger. Without anger in our hearts, all our thoughts and actions will be directed towards helping others, giving others convenience, confidence and hope. To attain such a level of practice is invaluable.

"Buddha nature is beyond time and limit." If we can rest our body and mind in actions, speech and thoughts that are free of all anger, then we will begin to see our limitless Buddha nature.

Remote mountains are safe havens for tigers.

The vast ocean collects water from all rivers.

Idle chatter gives rise to much gossip.

Troubles come from pushing too hard and beyond your means.

"Remote mountains are safe havens for tigers." You do not see tigers roaming the streets because they live deep in the hills, however this does not diminish the tigers' fearsomeness. A truly successful and mature person will not brag about his accomplishments, on the contrary, he humbly hides his ability and blends in with the ordinary folk.

"The vast ocean collects water from all rivers." Oceans, by their nature, accept water from all sources no matter how small. Never is a brook, stream or rivulet rejected. To be a great being you must become like the ocean, tolerant and embracing all beings.

"Idle chatter gives rise to much gossip." A lot of trouble in this world comes about from not minding our tongues. If we do not think before we speak and act we may create much conflict and adversity in the world around us.

"Troubles come from pushing too hard and beyond our means." Where do our troubles come from? Troubles often stem from our desire to be ahead of others and refusing to lose gracefully. On a deeper level, greed, anger, delusion, arrogance, doubt and deviant views are the six fundamental sources of human troubles.

The essence of this poem can be illustrated through the following way: Save your punches, save your energy. Save your tears, save your energy. If we cry too easily we just randomly release the energy from sadness and anger. If we can learn to hold back from spontaneous outbursts, we can channel the energy into tolerance for others. This way we can spare ourselves from much conflict with those around us.

When there is gossip about how should we deal with it? First, we should refrain from speaking so that we do not perpetuate it. Second, we should refrain from listening to it. Third, we should have no fear of it. There is gossip everyday, if we do not listen then there will be none. All gossip passes mouth to mouth in the context of the group. Why should we lower ourselves to the gossiper's mentality? We do not need to be too calculating or serious about it. Those who are incapable do not know how to handle gossip just like they do not know how to handle garbage. Gossip, like garbage, should not be taken too seriously. If it is not promptly disposed of it only fouls the environment and creates unpleasantness. Those who are capable use the three trainings (morality, meditation and wisdom) and the four boundless mindfulnesses (compassion, kindness, joyfulness and generosity) and naturally keep themselves above conflict and adversity.

A good doctor always finds out the cause of a sickness first.

Anger is quite harmful to someone who is sick.

Upon careful examination, a doctor then makes a correct diagnosis.

With the correct prescription, we can heal ourselves of our ignorance.

"A good doctor always finds out the cause of a sickness first. Anger is quite harmful to someone who is sick." Before a doctor can heal a patient, he has to find out the cause of the sickness so that he can give the right prescription. When someone is sick, anger can deteriorate their situation. If the patient can stay calm, he heals much faster.

The Buddha gave us eighty-four thousand ways to heal the eighty-four thousand troubles. For someone who is greedy, the Buddha teaches the meditation on filthiness. In contemplating all kinds of filth, naturally our greed will not arise. For someone who has a lot of hatred, the Buddha teaches the meditation on compassion. With the arising of the compassionate mind anger will not arise.

For someone who is ignorant, the Buddha teaches the meditation on dependent origination, or conditionality. We can then understand that all phenomena arise out of dependent origination. When we understand conditionality, we will see phenomena as so much flying dust and dirt and there will be no place for ignorance

For someone whose mind is scattered, the Buddha teaches the mindfulness of breathing to improve concentration. For someone who is self-centered, the Buddha teaches the contemplation of selflessness. These are the five meditations for settling the mind.

In ancient China there was a Ch'an master, Wu-chih, who gave this prescription for us to heal ourselves:

> *A section of a good gut, a piece of compassionate heart,*
> *Two taels of gentleness, three grains of justice,*
> *And don't forget integrity.*
> *A piece of directness, ten nuggets of filial respect,*
> *One gram of honesty, use all your good karma,*
> *And all the conveniences you can get.*

If we can use this prescription in our lives, we can gain a lot of ease.

"Upon careful examination, a doctor then makes a correct diagnosis. With the correct prescription, we can heal ourselves of our ignorance." It is only upon careful examination that a doctor can make a correct diagnosis and give the correct prescription. The six paramitas of Buddhism deliver sentient beings from the six kinds of sickness: generosity delivers us from greed, morality delivers us from wrong doing, tolerance delivers us from hatred, diligence delivers us from laziness, concentration delivers us from scattered mind, and wisdom delivers us from ignorance. These many prescriptions teach us how to be rid of the three poisons of greed, hatred and delusion. They deliver us from delusion and help us to attain Enlightenment.

The mountains and rivers will
one day cease to exist,

Form is ever changing, dependent upon
conditionality.

The lush mountains and the bubbling
streams

Can exist together through myriad
conditions.

In worldly life suspicion and jealousy

Will always keep people from living in
harmony.

Although the world is impermanent and ever changing, the law of cause and effect never changes. When *"The mountains and rivers will one day cease to exist,"* they do not disappear into nothingness. There is still the essence of mountains and rivers. Emptiness is a deep Buddhist concept that can be quite difficult to grasp. It is a wondrous "having". For all things there must be emptiness before we can have. Emptiness is potential. Take for example, a house must be empty before we can put furniture in it. The cup has to be empty before we can pour water into it. A bag has to be empty before it can hold things. Even our ears, mouths, noses, pores, and our internal organs have to be empty before life can exist. Do you think we can live if our eyes, ears, noses and mouths are all stuffed up?

That is why we say emptiness does exist, and this does not mean nothingness. It is because space is empty that we can have varying landscape. Some people do not understand the concept of emptiness. They think that emptiness is the opposite of substance. They think that substance cannot be empty, and emptiness cannot have any substance. As it turns out, emptiness and substance are opposite sides of the same coin. In the *Heart Sutra*, it is said that "Form does not differ from emptiness and emptiness does not differ from form."

Form is physical, while emptiness is mental. It is when we combine the physical (form) and the mental (emptiness) that all the different things in the universe arise. That is why we say, *"Form is ever-changing, dependent upon conditionality."* Emptiness is the true nature, the essence of all things, regardless of the form it takes.

"The lush mountains and the bubbling streams can exist together through myriad conditions. In worldly life suspicion and jealousy will always keep people from living in harmony." We have to understand that it is from emptiness that form exists. It is because of emptiness, and the right conditions, that the lush mountains and the bubbling streams can exist. When we deal with people, if we are suspicious and jealous, it is hard for others to accept us. We need to let go and cast off our doubts and envy. We should let our horizons expand and learn to be forgiving. If we are compassionate, we can be at ease and enjoy our life in this world.

There is nothing here that is worth our troubling over,

We should learn to overlook storms in a teacup.

We should get up from where we have fallen,

Then the whole world is ours to enjoy.

In this world, there is nothing here actually worth troubling over. A lot of our headaches are caused by our foolishness. The incapable will stir up troubles. A capable person will know how to eliminate troubles. Capable people know how to make a big problem into a small one and a small problem into no problem. The incapable, however, likes to fan the flame. When we deal with others, we should use gentle tact and not brute force. We should use compassion and not hatred.

When Alexander the Great led his army to try to conquer the world, he did not face much resistance. That is, until he reached the ocean. He looked at the ocean and sighed, "After all, man cannot conquer the entire world."

Although we cannot conquer the world, we can control ourselves. We need to overcome our selfishness, anger, and greed. If we can overcome our greed, hatred and delusion, we can then be liberated. The Dharma is always urging us to practice morality, concentration, and wisdom in order to put out the flames of greed, hatred, and delusion.

"There is nothing here that is worth our troubling over. We should learn to overlook storms in a teacup." In our daily lives, problems and headaches are unavoidable. Problems and headaches by themselves are not that terrible. All we need to learn is how to resolve them. We should learn how to make a big problem into a small one, and how to make small problems into no problem. If we hear something unpleasant, we should not repeat it, write about it or even think about it. Totally ignore it in body, speech and mind.

"We should get up from where we have fallen." In our daily lives, it is inevitable that we will be confronted with obstacles. We need to have determination, and get up from where we have fallen, then we can make progress. A lot of our heroes and leaders succeed because they are not afraid of failure. The founding father of modern China Dr. Sun failed again and again in his revolutions. He did not give up, and succeeded at last.

If we can have the determination in our practice of the Dharma, then we can conquer the army of defilements. *"Then the whole world is ours to enjoy."*

*It is not the ordinary man who can
bury his head in the snowy ridge,*

*Willing to give up the body for
the Dharma.*

It is only after bone-chilling cold

*That one can become a king of
the Dharma.*

When Bodhidharma came to the East, he practiced in seclusion at Shao Lin Temple. The Second Patriarch Hui-ko went to him to ask about the Dharma. During a long night of heavy snow, Hui-ko stood outside Bodhidharma's Ch'an hall waiting. The snow piled up to his knees, but Hui-ko did not budge, pleading Bodhidharma for his teachings.

Finally, Bodhidharma opened his eyes and asked, "What do you want standing here so long?" "Please, Master help me settle my mind." "Give me your mind, I'll settle it for you." "But I cannot find my mind." "I have already settled your mind for you completely." Once Hui-ko discovered his deluded mind, it became settled.

This is why it is said, *"It is not the ordinary man who can bury his head in the snowy ridge, willing to give up the body for the Dharma."* Standing in the snow pleading for the Dharma Hui-ko cut off his arm to make an offering. He was willing to give up his body for the Dharma and eventually he attained the Way.

Ch'an Master Fa-yuan came from the South. He traveled all the way to the North in search of the Dharma. On a cold winter night, he sat in the monastery's reception hall waiting to be admitted. No one paid him any heed from morning till night. The cold wind was fierce, and his companions left him, one by one, until he was all alone. The reception master then came out and scolded him, " It's so late now, why don't you just go?" And saying so he threw a basin of cold water onto Fa-yuan. Master Fa-yuan calmly and with dignity said, "Esteemed one, I have come from thousands of miles to learn the Way. Do you think you can chase me away with a basin of water?"

Master Fa-yuan was brave in his search of the Dharma. He tolerated all sorts of insults. Later, after he was finally admitted, he took some oil to cook noodles for the assembly of monks. The supervision master accused him of stealing temple's property to curry favor, and expelled him from the temple several times. Fa-yuan did not give up, he begged for alms outside to repay his debt to the temple. Eventually he was readmitted and was able to settle down. The depth of his practice was recognized by the temple and he was transmitted the Dharma.

"It is only after bone-chilling cold that one can become a king of the Dharma." Hui-ko and Fa-yuan went through many hardships which helped them to become the great patriarchs they became. Without the test of chilling cold, the plum blossom will not bloom. Without the heat of the hot summer, the lotus will not open.

The precepts are the best medicine for
the sickness of delusion.

We have to guard against the myriad
forms of suffering with

As much vigilance as if we were
protecting our own parents.

Eradicate delusion and ignite
the light of wisdom

To cross the bridge of life and death.

Use the bodhi raft to cross the limitless
ocean of karma.

"The precepts are the best medicine for the sickness of delusion." A country needs a system to establish itself. Abiding by the spirit of the law is most important. Buddhism emphasizes the practice of upholding the precepts. It is important to understand the spirit of the precepts, which one can always take to a deeper level. Apart from taking refuge in the Triple Gem Buddhists strive to uphold the five precepts which are: undertaking to abstain from killing; undertaking to abstain from stealing; undertaking to abstain from sexual misconduct; undertaking to abstain from false speech; and undertaking to abstain from taking intoxicants. If someone is able to uphold the five precepts, they will greatly nurture their life of wisdom which leads to enlightenment. If a family can uphold the five precepts they can find happiness living together. If a community or country can uphold the five precepts then everyone will become kind and saintly.

"We have to guard against the myriad forms of suffering with as much vigilance as if we were protecting our own parents." If we were all able to refrain from careless killing we would be respecting others' right to life. Not stealing means not transgressing on others' right to property. Abstaining from sexual misconduct means not to wrong our or others' physical bodies, good names or reputation through our sexuality. No false speech means not harming the honor and trust of both self and others. Through not taking intoxicants we protect our health so that our wisdom can remain alert. When we refrain from deluding and intoxicating ourselves, we can see the sublime in life.

Regardless of whether you are a Buddhist or not, everyone in this world can gain from observing the five precepts. If you want to live a long and healthy life you should not only abstain from killing living beings but also you should protect life or even liberate trapped animals. If you want to be wealthy, you should not only not steal and transgress on others' property, but you should also donate and give joyously. If you abstain from sexual misconduct, not only you but your partner and family will also gain respect by your actions. If you abstain from false speech and harming others verbally others too will not harm your reputation and trust. If you avoid intoxication naturally you will enjoy good health and alertness.

All this world's suffering and chaos come from people not abiding by the laws or upholding the five precepts. In society people are arrested and jailed mostly because they have violated the five precepts. If you wish to gain freedom, to eradicate delusion, to ignite the bright light of wisdom...if you wish to gain liberation from life and death, to ride the bodhi boat and cross the limitless ocean of karma then you will see that abiding by the five precepts is fundamental to human morality.

*May our bodies be continually
perfumed by the fragrance of the
precepts,*

*May we always be dressed
in the robes of samadhi,*

*Then the wondrous flowers of Bodhi
will perpetually surround us*

*And peace and joy shall be with us
wherever we find ourselves.*

"May our bodies be continually perfumed by the fragrance of the precepts." If we use the fragrance of the precepts to beautify our bodies, our behavior will be in accord with morality. See no evil, say no evil, hear no evil, and commit no evil. One must abstain from killing living creatures, taking what is not given, sexual misconduct, false speech and from taking intoxicants. Instead, one should free captured animals, give with joy, treat people with respect and decorum, praise others, and nurture the body and mind. In Buddhism, the Five Precepts, the Eight Precepts, the Ten Precepts and the Bodhisattva Precepts are all methods for beautifying and purifying the body and mind.

"May we always be dressed in the robes of samadhi." This sentence encourages us to practice meditation and attain samadhi. The attainment of samadhi can naturally sublimate our personality and ethics. In the past there were many old monks living in the monasteries, they spent several decades living in the Ch'an hall. Their nature was as lofty as the Mount Tai. They gradually attained this through the practice of Ch'an.

"Then the wondrous flowers of Bodhi will perpetually surround us." Along with the precepts and samadhi we must also develop bodhi wisdom. The flower of prajna are able to sublimate our being so that it may become one with truth. In this way, we may become true practitioners.

The wisdom of bodhi comes from initiative. Precept, concentration, serving others and our own cultivation; all of these require initiative. With initiative all things could be done well. Take for example, eating with initiative. When we eat with initiative the meal will taste particularly satisfying. When we sleep with initiative our sleep will be sweet and deep. In our affairs, if we do not have initiative we will be lacking in responsibility and we will not be respecting our jobs. We will also not be able to fully enjoy the company of others.

So we must use precept, concentration and wisdom to beautify our body and mind. *"And peace and joy shall be with us wherever we find ourselves."* By living simply anywhere we go we could be carefree all the time. In this way we could settle into the practice of precept, meditation and wisdom. Then we would truly be able to enjoy the peace and happiness of Dharma joy.

Only after the chilling cold

Will the winter plum blossom,
profuse in fragrance,

Only through the fiery heat of summer

Will the lotus flower release its sweet
smell.

"Only after the chilling cold will the winter plum blossom, profuse in fragrance." If we do not try hard, how can we achieve any success? As the saying goes, "no pain, no gain", we need to endure the tests of life before we can achieve success. The plum blossom is a winter plant and it is only after a bitter cold that it gives its sweet fragrance. Man should be like the plum blossom and learn to use difficult circumstances to enhance his own success.

"Only through the fiery heat of summer will the lotus flower release its sweet smell." We have to be able to live through the cold ice and snow of winter, and bear with the fiery heat of summer before we come through the trials and tribulations of life. In practicing Buddhism we have to be ready to go through many hardships. We should not expect smoothness in our endeavors. The mountains are full of peaks and the waves can be rough. In this world there are always things which go against ourselves. Therefore we have to plan our activities and be cautious in our thinking. We should be able to progress from setbacks and be like the lotus which flourishes in the mud; the hotter it gets the more fragrant it becomes.

We all have our strengths and we have to remember that all things happen for a reason and that our present is the cumulative effect of past causes. Just as the saying goes "when the going gets tough, the tough gets going," if we can persevere through the tough times, good times will be around the corner. All you need is to be patient, tolerant and not blaming others. In this way, you can discover the new world that is open to you.

In this complex society of ours, we will inevitably have to deal with numerous difficulties. We should be able to deal with losses and insults in order for us to turn the difficulties around to our benefit. We can turn failure into success. In times of darkness, as long as we have the light of the Dharma, then there is always happiness in our lives.

III. On Mind

◆

"Bodhidharma
came from the west
without a word,
Relying completely
on cultivation of the mind."

◆

Bodhidharma came from
the west without a word,

Relying completely on cultivation of
the mind.

If we want to write about self and
others;

Our brush would sooner dry out Tung
Ting Lake.

When Bodhidharma first came from India to China he brought with him no spoken or written word, only the Ch'an of the mind. This is why we say, *"Bodhidharma came from the west without a word."*

"Relying completely on cultivation of the mind." When Bodhidharma gave transmission, he did not play with words. He only relied on the contemplation of the mind. If we want to harvest the Dharma in our mind, we cannot just talk about it nor can we simply worship or join our palms. Instead, we have to contemplate and reflect whether we actually have compassion, tolerance, wisdom and the Dharma. *"If we want to write about self and others"*, and are stuck in rhetoric we are going down the wrong path. Language is only a means of expression, it is simply a bridge. It is neither truth nor Dharma. A picture of a cake cannot satisfy our hunger. If you simply understand the meaning of the words without realizing their truth in both your cultivation and behavior, then you are not a true practitioner of Ch'an.

"Our brush would sooner dry out Tung Ting Lake." Long ago an emperor set out a proclamation across the land that he would award twelve cows to anyone who can play his instrument for three days and three nights without rest. On seeing this proclamation, many musicians came to play. One in particular could sing and play exquisitely, in the hope of gaining the prize he played with all his might. After three days and nights, the emperor however did not keep his word and failed to reward the musician his prize. The musician was very unhappy and asked the emperor, "Why do you not follow through on your word as you promised?" At this the sovereign coldly replied, "Out of greed for the cows your playing was hysterical. You only gave the crowd an empty joy. I have not given you the cows so I only give empty joy. We owe each other nothing and neither of us took advantage of the other."

In practicing Ch'an we must have kindness, compassion, joy and generosity in our minds so that we can appreciate the real meaning of Bodhidharma coming from the west. Only then we can enter the ocean of Ch'an to sail freely. The empty joy of language is only a mirage, it is not the truth nor the ultimate.

With no real effort,
even wearing out the sitting mat,

There will be no realization of the
heart's true emptiness.

After great effort is applied,

Life will be like the flying colors of the
peach blossom in March.

"With no real effort, even wearing out the sitting mat, there will be no realization of the heart's true nature." If someone just pays attention to form and not substance, he will not be making much progress. He can be sitting there until his mat is worn out; yet if he does not apply himself, he will not gain enlightenment.

There is an old Chinese saying, "If your mind wanders while you recite Amitabha's name, you can chant until your voice is gone, yet you still will not make much progress." If we want to understand the Dharma, we must apply much effort. Just sitting down to meditate is not enough to understand Ch'an. When we recite Amitabha's name, we should use our hearts, not just our mouths. Likewise, to be successful in business we have to apply ourselves fully at the appropriate time. To practice the Dharma we must learn to cultivate both our mind and our actions.

In the movie industry, they give out awards not only to the main actors and actresses. They also give out awards to supporting actors, supporting actresses, set designers, costume designers, script writers etc. To produce a good movie, all these elements must be well coordinated. If any are absent, the quality of the movie will be diminished. This is aptly put in the common saying that, "Even a lotus flower needs green leaves to bring out its beauty."

On the stage of life, regardless of who we are, regardless of what roles we play, be it the main role or a supporting role, we have to do our part. We are all cogs in a wheel and only together can we attain a good end result. Regardless of what we do in this life if we act responsibly and cooperate with others, both in the family and at work, this is practicing Humanistic Buddhism. This is the true understanding of the Dharma.

"After great effort is applied, life will be like the flying colors of the peach blossom in March." We should all be true to our roles in life, and try our best regardless of how much money or intelligence we have. If we can all work hard without asking what is in it for me, then this world will be a pretty place, just like the peach blossoms in March.

An antique mirror can use a good polish;

It shines when the dust and dirt are removed.

We need to calm our wandering minds,

And find peace in our agitated heart.

"An antique mirror can use a good polish; it shines when the dust and dirt are removed." Our Buddha nature has been clouded by our clingings and cravings from our endless past. Just like an old mirror, it has lost its shine and luster. Restoring the shine of the mirror takes a lot of effort. Similarly, if we want to find our Buddha nature, we need to be willing to work hard.

How can we find our Buddha nature? We can recite the name of the Buddha and worship. We can meditate and we can practice the Dharma. What should we chant? We chant the name of the Buddha of the pure land. Why do we have to pay respect to Buddha? We use this method of chanting to control the delusions in the mind. What Buddha should we worship? Worship the Buddha of your own mind. Through worship we find our own Buddha that is inside of us. Similarly, meditation and practicing the Dharma will help us find our own self.

Just like we need to shower to keep the body clean, and we need to wash our clothes to keep them clean, when our hearts and minds have been filled with defilements we should cleanse them by chanting, worshipping and meditating. Once cleansed, the pure mind will be revealed, just like a polished mirror shines and reflects the true face.

"We need to calm our wandering minds, and find peace in our agitated heart." When you throw calmness into the confused mind, the confused mind will enter into calmness as well. We all have our delusion, confused thoughts and ignorance. We have to use right thought to correct these illusions. When we feel down and get angry easily we create a lot of irreparable damage, like the angry waves overturning a ship. Only when we are calm and peaceful, can we see the bright and pure self-nature. We can settle the confused mind and return to a peaceful state, feeling the openness of the universe and the bright sky.

Throughout the three time spans you
search for your mind, but see it you do not.

Your eyes look ahead of you but you
cannot see your own eyes.

You search for your lost sword where you
marked the waves,

In vain your eyes find nothing.

All the time we see what is unimportant,
wind, flowers, snow and the moon.

In searching for what we want we rarely find it. That which we do not want, however, is easily found. It is difficult to see what is true whereas deceptive falsehoods are always in front of our eyes. *"Throughout the three time spans you search for your mind, but see it you do not."* The three time spans in Buddhism are the past, present and future or variously the three lifetimes. The *Diamond Sutra* talks about, "past mind, present mind and future mind." We want to look for the mind in these three times. The past is already past and will not stay. The present mind is gone in a nanosecond and cannot be grasped. The future mind has not arisen yet and likewise cannot be held. This is why it is impossible and a waste of effort to look for the mind in the three time spans.

There is an ancient tale: long ago, there was a Ch'an master named De-san of northern China. He had heard of the Sixth Patriarch, Master Hui-neng who taught the sudden enlightenment practice. Arrogantly, Master De-san proclaimed that the southerners have no true Buddhism. Not willing to let go of this, he wrote a commentary on the *Diamond Sutra* and planned to go south to debate and criticize the doctrine of sudden enlightenment. He carried baskets full of his commentaries to the south. In the middle of his journey, he rested at an inn where an elderly lady made dim-sum. The old lady sensed his arrogant attitude and learned his reason for coming to the south, she said, "Ch'an master, I would like to ask you a question. If you can answer it, I will offer you my dim-sum for free. If not, then you need not bring your commentaries to the south." Master De-san thought little of the elderly woman and said, "Go ahead, ask anything!" The old woman asked, "In the *Diamond Sutra*, it says, the past mind cannot be found, the present mind cannot be grasped and the future mind cannot be detected. So, Ch'an master, you are eating dim-sum. What kind of mind is that?" The Ch'an master was at a loss for an answer. (In Chinese the words dim sum have more than one meaning. Dim also means referring to or pointing at. Sum also means mind and heart, the same like citta in Sanskrit.)

"Your two eyes look ahead of you but you cannot see your own eyes. You search for your lost sword where you marked the waves, in vain your eyes find nothing." Your precious sword fell into the river, and you marked the water where it fell thinking you could come back and find it. This is impossible. *"All the time we see what is unimportant, wind, flowers, snow and the moon."* If we are looking for reality we have a difficult search ahead of us. It is important to not be deluded by the external environment or deceived by our circumstances.

Fame and infamy have no standard,
let them be.

Ups and downs are one's fate,
don't blame others.

If we can learn to be humble,
our mind will be at ease.

With no attachments to extravagance,
our nature will be pure.

There are good and bad people. How can you tell a good person from a bad one? There is no set standard. Criminals will accuse a good person of being bad. A virtuous person will compliment a bad person on his good points. When a person gets a lot of praises, it will invite jealousy and slander. Look at a great person. If you believe in him, understand him, admire him, then he is a Buddha to you. However, if you do not understand him, do not trust him, then in your heart, he is a monster. Thus, Confucius saw everybody as virtuous, while a criminal sees everyone as a crook.

"Fame and infamy have no standard, let them be." Sometimes, neither our fame or infamy are well grounded. Do not be overly concerned with how others judge us, be it good or bad. If others praise me, it does not mean I am a good person. If others slander me, it does not mean I am a bad person. Some people slander others out of bad intentions. What can you do about this? Even the Buddha, in his lifetime, was slandered and harmed by his own cousin Devadatta. Not only did the slander not stick, it brought out the Buddha's compassion and greatness even more.

Without darkness, we cannot appreciate light. Without evil, we cannot appreciate virtue. Without bad people, we cannot appreciate good people. *"Ups and downs are one's fate, don't blame others."* When things are smooth, they are very smooth. When we have setbacks, the setbacks are numerous. Regardless what our situations are, we should not put the blame on others, not on our parents, nor on the gods. We have to understand that our current situation is the fruit of the seeds we sowed in the past. We have to realize that our destiny is within our control and the responsibility lies squarely on our own shoulders.

"If we can learn to be humble, our mind will be at ease." Once we recognize our true nature, we will know when is the best time to push forward, and when to retreat. Sometimes, we need to stand out to make a point; sometimes, we need to take a back seat. The key is to do what is best for the occasion. Then we will feel at ease with ourselves.

"With no attachments to extravagance, our nature will be pure." In this complex society, we need to have self-discipline. We should not cling to nor crave the temptations of this world. If we do not let our environment influence our Buddha nature, and work hard to build a pure land in this world, this will be a much nicer world to live in.

Through many Kalpas of
making offerings to the Buddha,

The merit accumulated from
making offerings is enormous,

When a thought of hatred
arises in our mind,

All merit will be incinerated to ashes.

"Through many Kalpas of making offerings to the Buddha." There are many ways of making offerings to the Buddha. For example, there are ten offerings: incense, flower, light, water, fruit, tea, food, jewels, prayers, and clothing. We may make offerings by paying reverence to the Buddha with our body, praising the Buddha with our speech, and contemplating the Buddha with our mind. We make four offerings: clothing, food, bedding and medicine to the Buddha. Or we may even make offerings with the seven treasures of the whole universe to the Buddha.

"The merit accumulated from making offerings is enormous." Though enormous, the merit gained from making offerings is nonetheless imperfect and exhaustible. *"When a thought of hatred arises in our mind, all the merit will be incinerated to ashes"* - as soon as the fire of hatred ignite in our mind, all the merit we have accumulated by making offerings will be burned off instantly.

Here is a story from the *Sutra of One Hundred Parables*:

Once upon a time there was a tortoise living in a pond. Because of a long drought, the pond completely dried up. The tortoise was so thirsty that he came to the brink of dying. Two wild geese felt sympathetic for the tortoise's situation. The two geese held a branch between their mouths, and the tortoise bit on the branch so the geese could take him to water. While they were flying in the air, the wild geese kept reminding the tortoise not to open his mouth under any circumstance, otherwise he would fall to the ground. When they flew by a village, a group of children saw the wild geese and the tortoise in the air and shouted, "Come look everybody! A tortoise was seized by two wild geese!"

When the tortoise heard the children's screaming and teasing, he became very angry. The tortoise thought, "I was not seized by these wild geese, they are just trying to take me to water." The tortoise thought that the children had falsely accused him and looked down on him, which made him very frustrated. The tortoise became very angry and shouted back to the children, "What on earth do you know..." No sooner when the tortoise opened its mouth then he began to fall from the air. He fell to the ground and died.

A lot of people will not admit defeat, instead they became angry, or jealous of other's success and upset over harsh comments. Living with a mind full of hatred is just like burning a fire in the wood of merit. Of course the merit would be entirely consumed.

When adversity comes,
it may be a cause of benefit.

When worldly friendships grow cold,
spiritual friendships open up.

Why should one compete with others in
the world of dreams?

Let the body and mind go,
and then one will see the world of truth.

This verse deals with two issues. First, when we have the willpower but lack physical ability, how should we face setbacks? When there is adversity, how do we deal with it? Adversity, actually, can be seen as a beneficial condition. The dangerous cliffs and mountains are a heaven for mountain climbers. The ever-changing sky is a paradise for aviators. When there is adversity we learn to be cautious, thinking of ways to overcome it. Adversity gives us the opportunity to transform a difficult situation into a beneficial environment.

Second, in human relations we generally wish that others would treat us warmly. When we are faced with coldness we may feel bad and get upset. Actually this should come as no surprise to us. Worldly relations are fickle and change suddenly as our situations change. While relations based on spiritual practice and the Dharma endure.

In the *Instruction Pertaining to the Royal Samadhi of Contemplating the Buddha*, it teaches us the following:

1. *Do not wish not to get sick. - If there is no sickness it is easy to become greedy.*
2. *In handling affairs, do not wish for lack of difficulties. - If there are no difficulties it is easy to become proud.*
3. *In understanding and exploring the mind, do not wish for a lack of obstacles. - If there are no obstacles, whatever we learn will be of little value.*
4. *In cultivation, do not wish for a lack of hindrances. - Without hindrances, our vows cannot be firm.*
5. *In work, do not wish to succeed easily. - If things come too easily we will not develop perseverance.*
6. *In making friends, do not use the friendship for your own benefit. - It is unethical to take advantage of a friendship for personal gain.*
7. *In dealing with others, do not expect them to yield to you all the time. When others continually yield to your wishes, your arrogance will grow.*
8. *When being charitable, do not expect it to be returned. - If we expect to be paid back we have an ulterior motive and are no longer practicing altruism.*
9. *Do not expect to share in others' profits. - If we expect to share in others' profits, our craving will be stirred.*
10. *Do not seek vindication when you are wronged. - If you seek vindication, your hatred and anger will grow.*

On the surface, these ten points seem to represent adversity, but actually they give us beneficial opportunities. In facing adverse conditions we are able to improve ourselves. These ten points refute normal ways of seeing human relations and bring us closer to living in accord with the Dharma. This is why the poem says, ***"Why should one compete with others in the world of dreams?"*** We have to let go of our body and mind, let go of our attachments and delusions and only then will we see a clear world, only then will we see the universe.

*The moment we change our minds,
we have Buddhahood.*

*Spring comes and the mountain flowers
blossom everywhere.*

So use compassionate hands

*To smooth and temper the minds of all
beings.*

"The moment we change our minds, we have Buddhahood." In practice it is most important to change delusion into enlightenment, to turn deluded action into skillful means. We need only change our mind gradually. If your mind can easily inverse greed, hatred and delusion into morality, concentration and wisdom then you will be able to change hell into heaven.

There was once an old woman who spent all her days crying over her two married daughters. The elder daughter married an umbrella salesman, the younger daughter married a noodle maker. Whenever the sun shone she thought of the daughter who sold umbrellas and worried that if no one bought her wares she and her husband could not make a living. Whenever it rained she worried that her younger daughter's noodles would not dry without the sun and deprive her of her living. So on sunny days she cried for her umbrella salesman's wife and on rainy days she cried for the noodle maker's wife. Month after month she passed her days crying and was known by all as the weeping lady.

One day , she met a Dharma master and told her she should turn her mind and change her point of view, "When the sun is out, think of your younger daughter's noodles. She'd be able to dry them quickly and sell a lot to support her family. Whenever it rains, your elder daughter's umbrellas will be in great demand and her family will prosper." The old woman suddenly realized the truth of this and switched her thoughts around. When it was sunny she smiled for the daughter selling noodles and when it rained she smiled for the daughter selling umbrellas. So all of a sudden the old woman was known not as the weeping lady but as the smiling woman. From that time onwards she was always happy and smiling.

A change in point of view has the power to turn the universe around and can transfer the common man into Tathagata. *"Spring comes and the mountain flowers blossom everywhere."* If we were able to change our circumstance, emotions and affairs, if we can transform darkness into light, and change adversity into ease, our hearts and minds would be clear and joyful. Would this not be a sort of spring?

"So use compassionate hands to smooth and temper the minds of all beings." Everyone of us has a pair of hands. Do not allow them to kill, steal, hit others or perform bad deeds. Change them into the hands of kindness, compassion, joy and generosity so that they can serve others and help others do good. The peace, harmony and joy of the world rely on our own compassionate hands.

The Buddha is in the spiritual mountain, don't go looking too far.

The spiritual mountain is right here in our hearts.

We all have this spiritual mountain pagoda within ourselves.

That is the true place of practice.

Where is Buddha? *"The Buddha is in the spiritual mountain, don't go looking too far."* This mountain is not any particular mountain. *"This mountain is right here in our hearts. We all have this spiritual mountain pagoda within ourselves."* Our own true Buddha nature is our pagoda. If we want to cultivate, we need to look within ourselves. *"That is the true place of practice."*

Once, there was a butcher that did not treat his mother very nicely, yet he was very devoted to Kuan Yin Bodhisattva. One day, he decided to make the long trip from his village to the famous temple on Mountain Pu Tuo. He had heard that this temple is a holy place and that Kuan Yin had appeared here on numerous occasions. Once he got to the temple, he looked everywhere to see if he could witness a miraculous appearance of the bodhisattva.

Not having seen the bodhisattva, he asked an old lady sitting by the road, "Where can I witness the miraculous appearance of Kuan Yin Bodhisattva?" The old lady smiled and replied, "If you want to witness that, you better go home. She is at your house right now." The butcher was shocked and asked, "Is it true? Is she now at my house?" The old lady replied earnestly, "Of course, it is true." The butcher then asked, "What does she look like?" The old lady said, "This is how you can recognize her. Kuan Yin Bodhisattva will be wearing her clothes inside out and her shoes will be on the wrong feet."

The butcher then hurried home. When he got home, it was already late at night. He knocked on the door and woke up his mother. His mother was afraid that her son would be impatient with her, so she hurriedly put on her shoes and clothes. She put on her clothes inside out and her shoes on the wrong feet. When she opened the door, the butcher saw his mom dressed like that and he fell on his knees and said, "Venerable Kuan Yin Bodhisattva." His mother was surprised and said, "What are you talking about? I am your mother, not Kuan Yin Bodhisattva." The butcher then replied, "When I was on my pilgrimage to Mountain Pu Tuo, someone told me that the person who is wearing the clothes inside out and the shoes on the wrong feet is Kuan Yin Bodhisattva."

If you are not respectful of your parents at home, what good is a pilgrimage? Kuan Yin Bodhisattva lives within ourselves. The Buddha lives within us. Being respectful to our parents, being compassionate and practicing the Dharma, this is the pagoda within ourselves.

IV Ch'an World

◆

"The search for Ch'an
took me far and wide,
Sleeping alone on a
rock with the clouds."

◆

The search for Ch'an took me far and
wide,

Sleeping alone on a rock with the
clouds.

The moon, on a windless night is
naturally pure;

In the rain, the green pines whisper
coldly.

"The search for Ch'an took me far and wide." Throughout time, countless Dharma practitioners would travel far and wide in their search for Ch'an and the truth. How did they live, how did they get by in their wandering cloud and water life?

Nowadays, to get a good job we need good skills and qualifications. Do not complain if you are not appreciated by others and given a responsible job. If you are not qualified it does not matter what the job is, you will not be able to do it well.

If you intend to travel far and wide in search of a teacher you would do well to take what comes your way. *"Sleeping alone on a rock with the clouds."* Without material greed, you will have no troubles. Even if you were to take one meal a day and sleep at the foot of a tree, you could still settle down and live peacefully, and be comfortable with what you have without being disturbed by your surroundings, be they good or bad. The white clouds in the sky above float free in space, this carefree cloud and water life is not bad.

The harder life is, and the more material difficulties you face, the more you will feel the Ch'an of the universe. You should have an open tolerant mind so that you can be at peace with whatever life brings to you.

"The moon on a windless night is naturally pure." On such a night the clear sky is especially bright and pure. If we cease from committing evil we will be able to stop the sources of confusion in the mind: right and wrong, good and bad, gain and loss. This will enable you to be at peace and with a pure character. *"In the rain, the green pines whisper coldly."* The cold sound is the sound of purity. Free from wrongdoings and the source of confusion, we can hear the sound of our own Samadhi.

In different periods of Chinese history, Venerable Masters Fa-hsien and Hsun-chuang were both pioneers in their search for the Dharma. They crossed the oceans and climbed mountains; they had enormous willpower which carried them through all sorts of sufferings and hardships. They were not deterred by their trials but persevered for the sake of the Dharma. The spirit of these two monks is illustrated in the following poem:

With one almsbowl the monk collected the donations of a thousand families

A lone monk travels ten thousand miles

All to gain an understanding of life and death

Begging for the Dharma and revealing the way to sentient beings spring and fall

Climb over mountains and cross over rivers,

If we can endure, our character will be toughened.

We will then see the intriguing benefits of persevering

And be able to deal with all kinds of situations.

Going through obstacles and solving problems can build our character. In fact, the tougher the problems, the better it is for our character. If we do not give up when we scale a mountain, we will eventually reach the peak and be able to feel the meaning of transcendency.

"Climb over mountains and cross over rivers," tell us that to reach perfection in Dharma practice often takes a long time. Some of the Ch'an masters spent many decades learning to understand Ch'an. Some spent decades in chanting. With time, their cultivation became perfected. We should have patience and not look for the shortest and easiest way. If we can "withstand the cold to clear the snow and withstand the heat to put out the fire," then we are ready to face difficulties. Things that come too easily can be lost easily too.

Thus, *"If we can endure, our character will be toughened."* If we can withstand ten years of trials in the cold then we can overcome a hundred setbacks and gain an unmovable foundation like a giant rock. If we have the wisdom and the courage to strive on even harder in the face of setbacks then *"We will be able to see the intriguing benefits of persevering and be able to deal with all kinds of situations."*

If we can be soft like water, then we can go through the densest bamboo thicket. If our spirits are as free as the clouds, even the highest mountains cannot stop us. If you serve others wholeheartedly and are not afraid of daily difficulties and obstacles, if you can tolerate all this then after the clouds are dispersed the bitterness will be gone and the sweet sun will appear with all the wonders of life.

In the Tang Dynasty, there was a Ch'an master by the name of Shih-te (meaning "pick up"). He was a well cultivated Ch'an master. When he first arrived at Kuo Ching Temple, he was not known by anyone and he was given housekeeping responsibilities, and only given leftovers to eat in the kitchen. He did this for a few decades. One day when they were reciting the precepts, Shih-te clapped and said, "Just pondering over these precepts, what good is it?" The chanting master reprimanded him, and he responded, "Wait a minute. One without hatred is moral. One who keeps his mind clean is like one who has renounced mundane life and joined the Sangha. Our natures are the same. There is no difference in all the Dharma." Those with morals will have multiple levels of experience and multiple levels of merit. This is not something that the impermanence and right and wrong of this world can limit.

When we deal with others, we should not only be able to withstand the gentle breeze of spring and the drizzling of summer, we should also know how to endure the cool frost of autumn and the ice and snow of winter. If we can endure the difficulties one by one, then a good and bright future will follow.

Each day the wind and moon flow into space.

From beyond the mountains the sounds of the bell and

The wooden fish harmonize with the breaking of the waves,

While the river flows by the moon's reflection stays still within its waters.

Yet the winds naturally carry the crash of the waves.

The white clouds in the sky flow with the wind to a distant land infinitely far away. The moonlight shines bright in the boundless starry sky. *"Each day the wind and moon flows into space."* From the first line we clearly see how the universe lasts while human life is brief. So while the sky seems infinite it is not everyday that we can appreciate the wind and moon.

"From beyond the mountains the sounds of the bell and the wooden fish harmonize with the breaking of the waves." From beyond the hills come the faint and fading sounds of the bell and wooden fish. They fall in with the rhythm of the waves. All is complete in beauty and harmony.

Living in the world our capabilities should correspond with our livelihoods. Our knowledge should suit our career. Our behavior should correspond with the Dharma. We should take interest in the world around us and have our pursuits match our environment. Just as the sounds of the bell and wooden fish are in tune with the waves creating a beautiful symphony. As long as our abilities, knowledge, and the capacity of our minds are in harmony with the community around us, our lives will proceed smoothly and our goals will be easily met. While at the same time we will get the support and praise of others

"While the river flows by the moon's reflection stays still within its waters." You have to take hold of yourself to avoid flowing along with the stream of things and forgetting yourself. You must have the fortitude to stay sober amidst a crowd of drunks. Even though there are thousands of people swept away by the current you must be able to remain firm.

"Yet the winds naturally carry the crash of the waves." The blowing winds bring the waves. When you understand your needs and conditions are ripe everything will be to your advantage. If you want to teach you need all the qualifications. If you want to get things done you need the right conditions. If you want to invest, you need to do the proper research and make a plan. If you prepare yourself fully you will naturally set up the proper conditions for your prosperity - just as the wind naturally carries the echo of the waves.

When theory and practice are balanced

There will be no conflict between self and other.

When the clouds are gone, there will be no shadows.

An ocean replenished from thousands of rivers never stops filling.

The vast space of the universe is my home.

"When theory and practice are balanced there will be no conflict between self and other." There are some people who are too practical. They are only concerned about immediate results and lack foresight to see the big picture. This is why they cannot have big achievements. There are others who can just give a good talk and lack substance. It is only when we can balance theory and practice that we can deal with all kinds of situations well.

In this human world we are used to looking at all phenomena dualistically, right and wrong, you and I, good and bad. With duality there is comparison and calculation. With comparison and calculation there will be gossip and adversity. When you balance theory and practice you will naturally get rid of duality and there will be no differentiation between self and other, right and wrong. Your mind will be open and naturally **"When the clouds are gone, there will be no shadows."** When you are able to rid your mind of duality and comparisons then you will have peace and equanimity in the world. There is a Ch'an saying, "the moment you stop thinking of good, you stop thinking of evil." That is enlightenment.

"An ocean replenished from thousands of rivers never stops filling." The reason that an ocean is vast is because it is non-discriminating. It gets its water from hundreds of rivers that empty into it. Similarly, the reason that the Mountain Tai can stand tall is because it is surrounded by other mountains, which keep it from erosion.

"The vast space of the universe is my home." What is the largest thing in the universe? It is its space. Its space can harbor everything, and does not hinder anything.

When Emperor Yuan-chang Chu was young, he was a novice monk for a short while. One night, when he returned to the temple too late, he was locked outside the gate. As he slept in the field, he composed this poem:

> The sky is my canopy, the earth is my blanket.
> The sun, moon and stars accompany me in my sleep.
> I dare not stretch out my legs at night
> Fearing that I might trample the sky at the end of the sea.

One who is open-minded can take all kinds of ups and downs. We should develop an open mind that is large enough to harbor everything and every circumstance like the great ocean and vast space. We should not reject others for differences in opinion. To be able to accept all kinds is the true essence of greatness.

The sun shines on the cloudless winter sky,

A westward wind brings clouds from the east.

You should tie the rope firmly,

And not drift aimlessly with the water.

"The sun shines on the cloudless winter sky." We all have Buddha nature. We have to look within ourselves to manifest our Buddha nature, just like the sun shining clear and bright in a cloudless winter sky.

"A westward wind brings clouds from the east." When the wind is blowing westward, it brings clouds from the east. This tells us not to overly react to external circumstances, be it good or bad, right or wrong. We need to know ourselves and do what we think is right. If we can maintain our Buddha nature, we can deal with all kinds of circumstances.

"You should tie the rope firmly, and not drift aimlessly with the water." Regardless of external changes, we need to maintain a balanced mind. We should not let our life drift away aimlessly. How can we maintain a balanced mind in the midst of all the temptations of this world? The answer lies in maintaining equanimity in all situations. We should maintain equanimity in the face of power and wealth, fame and honor. Money cannot change us, beauty cannot tempt us, never negotiate with the evil, never be moved by any slander. If we can do this, power, wealth, fame, and honor will not be able to control us. To take a step further, if we can anchor our mind on compassion and the Dharma, we will not drift aimlessly and lose control of ourselves.

In 1980, a model from California was paralyzed in a car accident. She was confined to a wheelchair. She noticed that her wheelchair was not well designed, so she asked two engineers to improve it. Out of compassion, she also shared her improved design with other handicapped people. She then started a wheelchair company which turned out to be a huge success. Within a few years, the company she started became one of the fastest growing companies in the state. From being a model that everyone admired to a paraplegic then to a successful entrepreneur, she gave us a good example how to have the confidence, patience and perseverance to control our destiny.

What does this verse tell us? It tells us that if we want to succeed in life, we have to depend on ourselves, to have resolve and not to let life drift away aimlessly.

Heaven and Earth where are they heading?

All the dust particles are illusive. What can we do?

Be it deep, be it shallow, let it be.

Water is water, waves are waves

"Heaven and Earth where are they heading? All the dust particles are illusive. What can we do?" Our universe, its rivers and mountains, its suns and moons, are all the result of the accumulation of dust particles. Where will the universe be if one day all the dust particles fall away? Where will we be? We all go through birth, aging, sickness, and death. Similarly, everything in this world goes through formation, existence, decay, and destruction. When everything has vanished, where will the universe be?

How does our universe come into being? Where do we come from? Where will we go to? Christians believe that God made heaven and earth. In Buddhism, we believe that everything is the result of dependent origination, or conditionality. Everything in this world goes through formation, existence, decay, and destruction. Destruction will in turn lead to formation, thereby, completing the cycle. Man, because he lives, will die. However, from death, we are reborn again, thereby completing the cycle.

"Be it deep, be it shallow, let it be. Water is water, waves are waves." Have you noticed that different people can have very different understanding of the same situation? We need to open our eyes and use our wisdom to really see. Be it deep, be it shallow, let it be. Do not be bothered by the opinions of others. The level of our own cultivation is what is most important.

In Buddhism, we often use the examples of "three animals crossing a river," and "three birds flying in the sky." When an elephant, a horse and a rabbit cross a river, regardless of the depth of the water, they each leave behind footprints of different depths. When an eagle, crow, and sparrow fly in the sky, though the sky is limitless, the three birds fly at different heights. We may all have different understanding of the truth; depending on each person's own ability. After all, we cannot deny that water is water, waves are waves.

What does this verse tell us? It tells us that in this impermanent world of ours, the best way of handling things is to have the understanding of the middle way.

The moon may be appearing half or full, yet it is still a complete moon.

If it is not dark to begin with, why wait for it to brighten?

The cool light shines from the past to now.

The beauty of our true nature glorifies the whole universe.

"The moon may be appearing half or full, yet it is still a complete moon." When we can only see a half moon, does it mean that there is only half a moon left? The moon is always full. It is just that we can only see half of it. Although we are drifting in the rounds of rebirths, our true Buddha nature has never been lost. It is always with us.

Once there was a group of blind people who wanted to know what an elephant looked like. So, they started to feel the elephant. Those who felt the trunk said that the elephant looked like a hook. Those who felt the ears said that the elephant looked like a fan. Those who felt the legs said that the elephant looked like a pillar. Those who felt the tail said that the elephant looked like a broom. Those who felt the belly said that the elephant looked like a big drum. What does an elephant really look like? Each blind person who felt part of an elephant only gave a partially correct answer. To find out what an elephant truly looks like, one must use wisdom to see the big picture. Similarly, in our daily lives, we usually only see part of reality, just like the half moon.

The moon is always full. *"If it is not dark to begin with, why wait for it to brighten?"* If we cannot see the moon at night, do we say that the moon does not exist anymore? If we do not know our true Buddha nature, does it mean that there is no Buddha nature?

The Sixth Patriarch Hui-neng achieved enlightenment when he understood the part in the *Diamond Sutra* which says, "We should develop the mind of intention without dwelling anywhere." Suddenly, he found his true Buddha nature. He gave out a sigh of astonishment, "Buddha nature is so clean. One's true nature can never be destroyed. Buddha nature is not movable. Buddha nature can manifest in many forms. Buddha nature is truly self-sufficient." Thus, Buddha nature is always bright and never dark; there is no need to seek another light.

"The cool light shines from the past to now." Buddha nature does not change. It is as old as eternity and yet it is always new. It shines from the past to now, and it is never used up or destroyed. *"The beauty of our true nature glorifies the whole universe."* Buddha nature is true, compassionate and beautiful. We should use our Buddha nature to shine on the three thousand worlds. Let us hope that the light can reach all the corners of the universe!

Everyone is his own being.

There is no need to plan for merit and glory.

The oriole sings in the gentle wind and warm sun,

Spring is already smiling at the flower buds.

"Everyone is his own being. There is no need to plan for merit and glory." When we practice the Dharma, the most important part is to find our true nature. As long as we know ourselves and examine our intentions, we can relax and be ourselves.

We can be happy from the mere praise from others. Our feelings may be hurt when someone looks at us askew. It seems that we are not living for ourselves but what others think of us. There are those people who are quite pretentious, their minds will be confined to their own fantasies. Others who are after money and glory are bound by fame and wealth.

"The oriole sings in the gentle wind and warm sun, spring is already smiling at the flower buds." The world can be a much better place if we can all find our true nature and turn our mind back to nature. When others need our compassion, we give freely. When others need our help, we give our service willingly. We should compliment others where credits are due. We should always try to help others whenever we can. If we know when to be kind and compassionate, when to be happy for others, and when to give, we can get along with others very well and will not be bounded or persuaded by anyone or anything.

True nature includes people and self, it benefits others and also self. If we can see that self and other are just the opposite sides of the same coin, the mind is then in the state of "The oriole sings in the gentle wind and warm sun." The sky is clear and the wind is gentle, birds singing, flowers blooming. We are at peace with ourselves and we feel good about ourselves.

There was a poem written in the Tang dynasty:

I searched everywhere for Spring,
But Spring is nowhere to be found.
Over the mountain I look, my shoes are worn,
I came back and coincidentally smelled the plum blossoms.
Then I know Spring is here, living among the branches.

Sometimes when we are set in our minds to look for something, it is nowhere to be found. If we do not calculate too much, do not mind the gain or loss too much, do not fantasize too much. Then strangely enough, the best results often happen naturally, like the water eventually becoming a river. Great merit is also achieved in this way.

The doors of the Dharma may be crowded, yet the devotees' minds are calm.

Look at the birds, they know when to leave the nest and when to return.

It is better to be without wants.

It requires higher morals to retreat than to proceed.

"The doors of the Dharma may be crowded, yet the devotees' minds are calm." People in the doors of the Dharma, though always coming and going and busy with work, keep their minds very calm. Their minds are placid but their bodies are active. Looking at the world we may see people who appear to be calmly sitting, but the troubles, worries, and attachments in their minds are multiple. These people are calm in body but not in mind.

In the Sangha there are many cultivated monks who travel about spreading the Dharma and benefiting sentient beings. It seems their activity is endless yet they often say that they have never left their original place. In Buddhism we should not look at people's external appearances without looking at their minds, nor should we look at their work without looking at them. Someone who can make things look easy while maintaining a busy schedule is possessed of a very calm and peaceful mind. .

"Look at the birds, they know when to leave the nest and when to return." Early in the morning, birds will leave their nests in search of food. As the evening draws near, you can also see them return to their nests for the night. Birds can find shelter within their nests. Where do we find our shelter? In this world, there are lots of people busy coming and going, not knowing when to stop. They are busy seeking wealth and fame; and not the ultimate shelter of their life. What a pity!

"It is better to be without wants." I do not pursue fame so I do not rely on others. In this way my character is naturally sublime. I do not crave wealth because inside myself I always have endless treasures, wisdom and abundant merit. There is nothing missing in my world. I lack only external craving. I enjoy giving and being charitable. Without wants one has high morals. Wanting brings greed, not wanting is the highest form of Dharma joy.

"It requires higher morals to retreat than to proceed." Some people just know how to run forward; they do not know that once in a while, one has to retreat. Do not confuse retreating with passivity. Look at the fearsome tiger, it retreats before it pounces. We have to stoop before we can leap. It is easier to push forward, however, it takes a lot of discipline to retreat and let others go first. Thus, we have to remember that we have to retreat before we can proceed. Such conduct will not only enhance our integrity but also help us move ahead on the path of the bodhisattvas.

Fo Guang Shan
International Translation Center

In view of the ever increasing interest in learning Buddhism in the Western world, Venerable Master Hsing Yun established the Fo Guang Shan International Translation Center in 1996. Works on a wide spectrum of topics had since been translated into English, Spanish, German, French, Russian and a number of other languages. Free English monthly booklets on various Buddhist topics are published for distribution in the branch temples of English speaking countries.

Some of the booklets published include *Nirvana, Conditionality: The Law of Cause and Effect, Speaking of You and Me, Living the Dharma, When We See Clearly.* Other publications include *Humble Table, Wise Fare (Parts I & II), The Carefree Life, Being Good* and *Only A Great Rain.*

We appreciate any comments or suggestions that you may have toward our publications. You may forward your comments and suggestions to:

Fo Guang Shan International Translation Center
3456, South Glenmark Drive, Hacienda Heights,
CA 91745, U.S.A.
Phone: (626) 923-5151
Fax: (626) 369-1944
Email: itc@blia.org

Other English Publications
by Venerable Master Hsing Yun

1. *Hsing Yun Ch'an Talk*
2. *Perfectly Willing*
3. *Happily Ever After*
4. *How I Practice Humanistic Buddhism*
5. *Where is Your Buddha Nature?*
6. *Being Good: Buddhist Ethics for Everyday Life*
7. *Only A Great Rain: A Guide to Chinese Buddhist Meditation*
8. *The Carefree Life*
9. *Humble Table, Wise Fare: Hospitality for the Heart (I)*
10. *Humble Table, Wise Fare: Hospitality for the Heart (II)*
11. *Cloud and Water: An Interpretation of Ch'an Poems*
12. *Lotus in A Stream: Basic Buddhism for Beginners*

If you would like more information regarding these publications or interested in ordering the above titles, you may contact us at: Phone: (626) 961-9697
Fax: (626) 369-1944
Email: itc@blia.org